The Singer, The Lesbian, & The One With The Feet: 69 Bipolar Love Poems

Justin Booth

Cowboy Buddha Publishing, LLC

Cover Photo by Tucker Martin
Model: Aimee Stockton

Cover & Book Design by Jessica Dyer
Illustrations by Justin Booth
Publishing Logo by Ted Nichols

February 2015

Cowboy Buddha Publishing, LLC
Benton, Arkansas

Cowboy Buddha
PUBLISHING

I dedicate this book to the muses; to Theresa, Saira, Tina, Anna, Hannah, Steph, Laura, Heather, Kara, Daniela, and Darla. Also Alicia, Martha, Pamela, Alexandra, Sreemanti Sengupta, Cheryl, Sandy, Tami, Fiona, and the other Kara. Tracy, Judy, Kelly, and Ruth. To that cocktail waitress outside of San Antonio (you know who you are). To Carla, and Allison and Lisa and Sammi, and the tattooed girls, the subs, and the ones who text pictures, Gina Nemo, Annie, and the redheads in Ireland. Of course to Sylva, all of the Paulas, most of the Amys, and to Aimee – god knows I love you. To Lynne, and Michelle, my ex-wives, girlfriends and the girls on the stroll. To Jen, Darcie, Robbin, and Chloe. To Kara Bibb's mom, and the ones whose names escape me …

and to Felicia.

– Justin

CONTENTS

INTRODUCTION

Outlaw junkie homeless guys, hookers, praise band singers – pretty much everybody falls in love. The poems I have put together in this collection span the entire time I have been serious about my writing. They may not portray the kinds of things you think of when you think of love poetry. Some are about longing and passion, others about the kick-to-the-gut pain of unrequited love. They are genuine and from that place that each of us has inside. I hope they move you in some way, just as I am moved by the wonderful women who have become my muses and more.
God help me, I loved them all.

– **Justin Booth**

FALL

I refuse to fall
for you
like something
from a clumsy
childhood dive
into a chat driveway
tearing my pants
and digging
little grey rocks
from my hands after
and then the red stuff
that burns.
(This is gonna
sting a little.)

I refuse to fall
for a(nother)
25-year-old girl
with smokey eyes,
slender wrists,
and ankles that
fit perfect
in my hands.

Please.

I refuse to fall
for golden brown skin
freckled just below
collar bones that
seem carved by God

if he were an artist
like Picasso who
continued to fall
in baby-making love
with girls terribly young
and beautiful as you
until he died.

I refuse even if
you pour me whiskeys
and tell me that
you support my writing
and wear my face
on white panties
next to your
oh my goodness.

I refuse to,

even if you are
my first coffee smile
and my hope I dream
as I lay myself down
to sleep.

I refuse to fall in love with you
(or even write you a poem).

NEW FRIEND

The sun shines
through plate glass
warming the openness
lighting perfectly
the space.

Conversation
easy as falling
maple seed,
floating, drifting,
wafting in gentle
breeze.

Smiles and laughter-
secrets and tears.

New friends with
thousand year souls.

OLD FOOL

Here we go again.

Another beauty
and half your age.

She loves poetry-
She writes.

She paints-
She tells you
your stuff is good.

She is absolutely
the most stunning creature-
she's half your age.

You both love art
and sex and poetry
and Manu Chao
and all things Japanese

she laughs at
your jokes
and gives strength
to your tears.

Another beauty
and half your age.
Here we go again.

SUMMERS

On days that the unit
would chug and hum
in a battle against
mid-day heat its
valor no equal to ability.

We would wake long
before we wanted and
we would fix knowing
that would mean an extra
one to cop that night.

Sometimes there would
still be a bottle and
we would drink brown
from the plastic cups
that came with clean towels,
from Flo's cart.

It was the closest we came,
ever, to being us. People.
To having conversations,
the regular kind or
at least how we imagined.

I told her I wished I loved her.

She asked if I knew
any games that didn't feature death.

BAD BREAKFAST AT IHOP AND FALLING IN LOVE

"Could be
one of them
Catfish"
slurping coffee
with an
accusing flair.

I looked for
the polyester
betty who had
taken our order
and faded away
into IHOP
hell.

"You know like
that ball player-
the Samoan
kid and the
queer"

I screwed up
my face,
"First of all
you're a dick,
and second-
the fuck are
you talking
about"

"You say this

chick did T.V.,
she's a singer
and such.
Jesus just look
at that picture-
so outta your
league"

"Her dad's
some famous
beatnik dude
that kicked it
with Frank"

The hard edged
waitress
whose mouth
remained twisted
into a speed-fueled
grimace
fairly threw
plates with
bacon and eggs,
burnt hash browns
and tweaked
out of sight
before I could
ask for
Tabasco.

"Have you ever
seen this broad,
you know
face to face?"

My head ached
and my stomach
did back flips
at the sight
of egg yolks.

"Does she know
you got nothing,
she know you
did time?"

Not for the first
time I thought
that booze made
for strange
company, and
leaned back
and belched.

"There's no way
to tell you,
that you'd
understand-

first you're
a dick,
and second
she writes me
these love poems-

she's
shown me her
soul."

I bent over
the bad breakfast
and ignored
the look
he gave-

it sounded dumb
even to me
but I loved
falling in love-

and do not poke bears.

A BOONES FARM SONG
serenades us

as we stand outside

a mom and pop store

in the same

neighborhood

that our parents

first kissed

it's hard to dance

When you're

drunk and there

is no music

but we would

be in love

so very

badly

lustful youth

lingering kisses

sidewalks

and spring

PAULA

Things don't happen by chance,
that's what she said
When we inexplicably became
Facebook friends.
I followed her link to a site
and saw her paintings.
And photos.

I saw her heart.

I never do this sort of thing.
I've never chatted with a stranger.
She had the bluest eyes,
the funniest way of talking,
she had a tortured past.

I had an adult beverage,

and unlimited minutes.

We talked every night for hours
like two teens who'd never loved
And she came to visit once.
She brought paints and poems
and a great glass for drinking.

It was like striking a wooden match
to life, bursting brilliant with flame.
But I dropped it before the burn,
a little scared I guess, and

I haven't seen her since.

HAVING FALLEN IN LOVE

There had been women.
Some of them
said they loved me.

I guess some of them
I even loved,

but I had never
fallen in love
until I was
nearly fifty years old

She seemed perfect.

We met at a freaky
little hippy church
downtown and she was
sunshine, she was fire.

I asked her if
she would let me
write love for her,
smiling she said
yes to me and
I gave her my heart.

On Tuesdays we would
paint in plate glass light
and listen to music
and sometimes our
fingers would touch

or she would tussle
my hair and I would
be drunk from her

presence. I fell in love
with her in that way
that only the most
foolish hearts can know.

When she was through
with me I wanted to die,
and others could see it,
people waited for it to
happen in that peculiar
way that morbid racecar
fans wait for mortal crashes.

But I didn't kill myself,
there was no need,

for having known the
elation of falling deeply
in love like that then
having it snatched
away was like

not being alive

anymore. Suicide
would just be redundant.

ON A PUDDLE OF WATER

I was stoned,
in love
a thousand rains
ago.
Hundreds of
dark clouds
opening,
sunlight
creeping through.

Thick as a brick
skin now,
face set sure as
concrete.

Wrinkles,
eyes weighed
heavy with bags,

and moles and
other skin things,

teeth bad,
and a storm
is stirring, but I
just might love
a barroom girl

Pretty as sunlight
on a puddle,
so I go on.

Pretty as sunlight
on a puddle of water
I am stoned in love
so I go on
taking chances
on sunshine
on late Spring

THE THERAPIST

I click my rings together
and stare at her open toe
shoes under her desk,
her tiny feet.

She is taking notes
or facebooking I cannot
really tell from the click
of the keys.

I look up quickly
and steal a glimpse of her
before turning my gaze
to the window.

"So not much writing this week?"

She does her best to engage me-
To pull me from this
Tony Soprano fantasy
spinning out in my head.

"No mostly this week I just wanted to die."

"Which one was it?"

"Huh?"

"The singer, the lesbian, or the one with the feet?"

"They all have feet."

I look at the walls,
my bag in the floor,
the ceiling- count the tiles
then slowly back to her.

She is the skull faced chick
from Day of the Dead art.

She is a 10th grade lab partner,
too pretty to speak to until now.

Blessed Mary, Mother of God
and Divine Listener of my Tales,

official laugher of my jokes.

She digs my poems and I love her smile.
This therapy thing may not work out but
I think I will give it a couple of more weeks.

BURN FOR YOU

I get them
mixed-up,
confuse
dinosaurs
for dragons,

dragons
for dirty
white girls
in tank tops
rolling
drop tops,

and them
for the
devil

but only
after.

I come from
pitch night
terror
and troubles
that trump
tender tendrils
of goodness
and god

but I would
burn the world

down
just to give
you a bucket
of ashes

if that
is what
you want.

I would throw
old people,
the handicapped,
aside in
burning
stacked-brick
building
to save you,

I would
smother
the breath
of your lover
if you
nodded and
told me to...

I would commit murder,
treason,
and heresy,

blasphemy.

Anathema?

I will be that
and more

I would slap

at angels like
mosquitoes and
kick deities
in the ass
like mouthy
cowards afraid
of what I might
do.

I would fly
into fiery fate
with you,

if you would but choose.

I would fight God
for you

and lose.

A BROKEN HEARTED LIFE

They
say you can
die

of a
broken
heart

she
said to me
once

but

I
am more
likely

to get
hit by a
car

We were
castaway people
from the

other side
of the
glass

she
had lived

a crumpled
dollar bill life

like
a tattoo
on Downtowns
arm

her
kisses tasted
like

lipstick and
vodka

I
was thinking
about

a sober Chistmas
but
she just

shook
her head

She
had hardluck
blues

Quality
House liters
the only cure

When
I would
leave
her,
to walk the
eight blocks

her
face would be grey
as a cypress barn

When

I would
come back from
day labor

mornings

with
the brown paper
package

her
eyes would light
up like

I
just got out
of prison

I
see her

still

a thousand faces

sad old ladies

giddy little girls

she
was the saddest
muse

she
died of a
broken heart

70 AND 50

When I am seventy
and you are fifty,
will you
think of me?

When my skin is
mottled and eyes
are gone

will you

still know me
then.

Will your thoughts
turn to me on the
occasion that you
smell cigarette smoke

or hear a song?

When you are
fifty
and I have turned
seventy

will you doubt
still the love
of ten

thousand
poems.

Or will you
smile and remember
how you moved
me and shaped
my words.

A DECENT POEM

My hair would be
standing out long
in all directions.

Rolling Rock
bottles like dead
men at my feet.

She would be
cleaning, organizing,
whirling in all

directions.

I'd be watching
the television
not listening,

thinking about
the things I wanted
to say eternal.

I want a house,
I want babies,
I want to make
a difference in
peoples lives,
she'd say.

I'd nod,
and scratch
and smoke a butt.

I just wanted
to write a
decent poem.

ORIGAMI

I watched him
from outside,
some place
that was foreign

far

but afforded
scrutiny.

Around the
world,
scurrying
from places
darker than
Hamelin
and sadder than
Hank's holiday
trees,

than Plath's
Bell Jar-
they reached out.

And having
no
less power
than
to take on
their pain,

he folded
the sadness-
the
childhood
sufferings,
the cold love
neglect,
the late night
dates
with broken
open razors-

he took it
in his hands,
and creasing
and shaping
turned them
into
little works
of art.

A crane, a butterfly, a dragon.

Folded despair
and the past and slipped it
into his own breast pocket
and kept it there.

From where I stood
outside of that world
I could not say that
he changed them

but even I could
see
how sexy the relief.

TO BE SAD

The asphalt
parking lot
a rainbow
of petroleum
sheen
on this mornings
fallen rain,
a train whistle
crying
from a long
time ago.

The news print
sky still
sore from
its passion,
and something
in all this
bears a sense
of nostalgia
that gives
me pause.

Struggling against
the past,
like bad nicknames
or Chinese
finger cuffs,
sticks me,

like cartoon
quicksand, my
greatest
childhood fear.

I worry this day,
but not of days gone.

I worry that
in Dublin
they'll laugh
at me,
calling me
the gobshite son
of Billys
gone over.

That appalachian
poets who
drive hacks now
in New York
will find me
esoteric, and
ask if I read.

That whiskey
voiced girls
cut from
misogynist cloth
will
dismiss me
quickly,
a dog and
pony show
who'd rather
get high.

On prison grey
mornings,

all these
things cause me
concern,
but mostly I fear
that one day
I will meet

Her

and I will
no longer be
able
to be sad.

If I meet

Her

will I ever
be happy to
write?

MAGIC

Dozing off,
whether from
the hour or the
Rolling Rocks,
I missed her last
question-

How do you
know it's magic?

How do I explain
the sense of gravity,
the pulling force
that drew me
as I saw her that
first time?

How can I say
to her
that the world
and those things greater
beyond it really
rarely puts two
spirits in circumstances
allowing them
to know that they
already share love

of art and song-
that the power of

words
strung together
in wonderful synchronicity
move the both of them

in ways deeper
than most can fathom.

Beauty certainly,
but more in the spell,
inspiration and creation
so much more
than lust.

Lust though,
remains.

The most magic
thing of all, this

relationship between poet and muse.

Magic and beauty
and lust and love-

and only a
supernatural universe
can offer your answer,

or me my muse.

LIKE A JIM CROCE SONG

There are photographs
in the attic
of my mind.
Old black and whites
and some
in sepia tones.

They are moments
captured from
inky shadows,
memories of the
days when I was
a better man.

Now I am
somebody else.

There are pictures
in sticky page albums
but they exist
only in my dreams,

I have surrendered
the luxury of possessions
as delicate as these,
subject to curling
from the heat,
mildew on rain soaked
days spent moving

too tired to

sit still.

The attic of my mind
saves the happiest moments;
the birth of a child,
a wedding, potluck
lunches at Grandma's
house on Sunday
afternoons, snapshots of
young love
in a wooded park...

Nights alone I sit
and leaf through them
sometimes
trying to remember
sometimes
trying to forget.

CRAZY DEB NEEDS A NEW PAIR OF SHOES

crazy deb was
a prom queen
gone bad
and she stood
  and cried
and prayed
one day like
she had
learned in vacation
bible school
all that time
ago over
tuna sandwiches
  and red
kool aid
jesus what
she wouldnt do
for a hit of dope
but god didnt care
or the tricks were scared
so she went
back to the
little room
where she stayed
and stared
on better days
at the
soiled curtains
and black greasy hand
stains
around the

doorknob door
and shadows
in the corners
and the pulls
on the drawers
unblinking
thinking of the
tattered carpet floor
and her scuffed soled
shoes by the bathroom
were tired and ready
to sleep
and they were
sick of getting high
and beating
down the street
or flying
near her ears
on her toe curled feet
so
they kicked back and settled
down
while the crazy prom queen
came unwound

BLACK MUSE

My muse,
the one who
lives
inside of me,
has gone
Dark.

She is mad.

She no longer
shares
her tales
of love
with me.

She speaks
in breathy
whispers
of heartache,

she dares me
to die,
to pen a poetic
last note
and leave
my words
behind.

She laughs
at my pain.

She does not
know
that she remains
my Muse,

that there
is beauty still,
in the sadness.

There is art
in my
brokenness.

The tearing away
at a man
by the
blackest Muse,

is still
better than
no muse

at all.

SMOKE RINGS IN THE DARK

Lightning hopscotches
across a morose sky
and smoke rings
crash like the surf
against the ceiling
above my bed,

my only company.

I think of the day
and the wicked angels

smile,

and carefree way
that she carries
herself,

the subtle curve
of her form.

I smile at the thought
of her,
laugh aloud at
the things she has
said.

I am jealous of
her boon companions:
Disappointment, Sadness.

Happy though that
they are common friends.

A storm blows in
and I crush out a smoke,
and lightning strikes again.

THE VALUE OF POETRY

In my senior year
Of High School
I met her and
She smiled
She studied English
Or rather how to teach it
At the local
University
I was quite smitten
Taken with her
She asked us to write
So I did
I wrote stories
And she read them
Poems and she giggled
I tried to be provocative
In puberty's most
painful/beautiful way I held
books low and center
while we spoke
When she left
Eventually
I learned life's
Most valuable Lesson
Love is bittersweet
They all go eventually
And even bad poetry
Can get you laid

DREAM LOVERS DIE

We were headed
to see the art
a couple of blocks
over, the first
time I rode in
her car.

What kind of music,

she asked and
without a thought
of how cool she was
or even the difference
in our ages I said,

Hillbilly.

She put in some Townes
and I fell in something
with her right then.

MAYBE BETTER

The second
time I saw her
she walked
into my room
and saw
the mattress
on the floor
and said Jesus
Christ
you still live
like a hobo.

She threw
down
a canvas
messenger
bag filled with
protest pamphlets,
and porn from
Holland and
poems by
Baudelaire

then kicked
off her shoes,
Tom's,
and pulled
a shapeless
cotton dress
up and over
her head

and slipped
into bed next
to me.

Twenty and three
my junior
her skin was
cream and goodness
her hair
the color of
an Irish girl
named Maggie's,
her eyes of green
had already
given up
tears.

Do you have a drink?
she asked
and I passed
her what I had.
I am not
like the others,
she said,
not sad
or lonely

I am a writer,
a poet,
like you,
but better.
It was the closest
I had been to loving
in a long time.

We wrote a hell
of a story
before she
moved on.
She was a writer
and maybe
a little broken,
maybe better.

FOR SALLY GRAHAM

She had a face
that said golden,
southern girl,
and eyes
that smiled
at how much
smarter
she was
than the rest
of the world
though she
would never
say it.

It would never
pass her
cherubic lips.
I can imagine
that she might
weep at
renaissance paintings
but doubt
that a mortal man
could cause the same.

Gemini's daughter
captures me
in a spell
then releases me
just as quickly
and laughs,

and I am forced
to laugh with her,
her charm is such.

Having conquered
stage and small screen,
the tallest of Gotham,
and been courted
by Kings
on faraway continents,
who am I
to love her.

Someday maybe,
though,
I will try.

THE LAST

This is the last
love poem
I will write
for you.

Four A.M.
and I cannot
recall the words
of the poem
I dreamed,

though I
remember the
small printed
ink and
the way I
hurried it down
in a stenographer's
note pad
across the
paint splattered
table from
you, and the
doughnut holes
that you brought
me every
Tuesday in
that ridiculous
car that you
have driven
since high school.

I sit awake
searching for
the words
that came
so easily in
my slumber causing
you
pause,
to give me
head cocked
smiles of
adoration.

I strain to
remember
the words or
even the
feelings, even
the love. I
am angered
at the loss.

This is the last
love poem
that I will
write you,
though I
promised you
10,000,

it is only
me that cares
and I send

them out
empty,
a death
not fitting
poetry or
love songs
written at
four A.M..

This is the last,
love poem
I will
write.

THE FRANZIA CORRELATION

Neon glow
accented smiles
and clever
talk of
writers and
soft serve
politics.

Barefoot Moscato
philosophers
telling me
about Travon
and I wonder
if all the
ones who still
have hope
and great asses
ever get
the news
anywhere but
Facebook.

One more
bourbon
followed by
one more
beer followed
by one more
heart felt
nod, to justice

and Mother Nature,
and equality
for all.

Finally she asks to see my place,
and we stop
at the liquor store
on the corner.

I grab a
cardboard
container
of Franzia and
wonder if
the shitty wine
in the
throwaway
box
isn't some kind
of metaphor
for the love
I make.

ONE

Photographs,

women I have loved
hang framed
and glass covered
among
half finished paintings
and 33 1/3 speed
collections
of folk and country
sounds.

Mixed with group
shots of
dead poets from
college and
closeups
of pretty
tattooed feet,
toes spread wide.

Snapshots of past
lovers, a two year
old calendar and
a couple of columns
by Koon and
one of those magnet
and metal filing games
you got as a
party favor when
you were a kid.

This one looks
like Chloe.

I keep the photos
of the old ones and
the new ones don't
mind.

They know.

I only really
loved the one.

What are a few framed
memories after they
have already laid in bed
with me and listened
as I talked about the
one.

I'D PRETEND TO CUT OFF AN EAR

Some people say I went mad in May,
but I am sure it's been longer than that.

Next came the free advice;
peanut gallery, and all that.

Everybody kept saying,
'Let her go'
'you need to get over her'
I would nod
say 'Yeah sure'
'you're right.'

I didn't,

didn't even want to,
blew two different
chances with two
completely wonderful
women probably
still wondering-

still shaking their pretty heads.

The first would do things
for me in bed,
amazing things, not for
the first time but
in new and phenomenal ways.

The second was an L.A. gal
who'd grown up in the biz;
had done t.v., knew Johnny Depp
and Slash's accountant,
said she loved me in other lives
and
offered me a book deal.

I just couldn't focus
on those things yet,
this was some sad poet
stuff for real and I was
Nine Thousand poems
in the hole.

Truth is a girl like her
deserves some coo coo ca choo.

A girl like her-

once in a lifetime-

she needed to see
how crazy in love she
had made me,

I owed her that much,
the way she made me feel.
The things I wrote.

She had given me
back forfeited passion

it seemed only fair
that I stand in white T-shirted
downpours crying out
her name in the hope
of love's resurrection
fashioned from audible anguish.

A muse like that,
you've got to write the sad ones too.
Love poems can't compare.

My ears long deaf and heart hardened
against those who advise 'get past her'.
I think to myself-
not while the words still come.

Not now or anytime soon.

A girl like that deserves some crazy poet shit
to think about
for the rest of her life
when every real thing has lost its groove.

HEART AND SOUL

My words,
yes,
that is what
drew you,

that sparked
a remembrance
of connections
long ago.

A dream,
since,
that is what
made you

yearn for
a love shelved
a moment
'til destiny's
deja vu.

Your poems,
love,
they are
treasured

they are
written in
ancient ink
onto my
heart and soul.

COOL BREEZE

No
Tangle of Words
Of Mine
Suffice
I Try
In Vain To
Tell Her
She Is
SUNSHINE
She is
A SMILE
Spread Broadly Across
My Weathered Face
She Makes
My Mistakes
Seem Adventures
My Doubts
And Weakness
Human
She Is
So Much More
SHE IS SUNSHINE
SHE IS A SMILE
No Jumble
Of Syntax
I Own
Will Do
I Cannot
Put It Into
Verse

She Is
A COOL BREEZE
She Is
AN ANGEL
Wings Flapping Madly

At My Jokes Sometimes
My Demons
And Darkness
Just Stories
She Is A Cool Breeze Angel
Singing Hymns Of New Sin Shared

THE TATTOO

The tattoo
that I got
long ago,
faded now,
I can still feel
the scarring
of its design.
The colors
dim
edges blurred
hardly
do I remember
why
I felt
compelled
to announce
to anyone
who saw me
shirtless
that you
were
mine forever.
Fat throwback
Sailor Jerry
letters pricked
into skin.
I touch it
tracing the path
of late night
artist's
staccato hand

thinking back
to your smiling
freckled face.
Eighteen
fresh from home
full of
expectation
and rebellion
ready to prove
yourself and
trust me.
You are long gone
now, but the
scar, and memory
remain, linger
as dust motes
float upward
in sunbeams
slashing a
motel comforter
and a yellowed
photograph of
that other time
when we were us
and two kids
walked
arm in arm
in sidewalk's
neon glow
ready
to take on
the world.

AGAIN

And just as the sun begins,
in frozen yogurt hues,
the third hand car with its
grinding clutch and
its squeaking brakes
rounds the corner
creeping guiltily home
and she is relieved that
he is not dead
or locked up in jail.
She stands in the open
doorway hurt and angry and
scared that he'll never
quit binging and grow up
to be a father to the boy.
That the next may be the last.

She slams the door shut.

This is it then, he thinks,
she will leave me. This is the
last time, I swear it.

One last chance.
He is sorry
again.

You're so special? You're sad!
You can't stand to be with me?

I see it coming you know...
I am not stupid, just because
I don't say....
Tortured soul artist? So...
special? You hurt us-
you hurt me. Nobody even reads that
shit but me.
Come to bed, I love you.

And so it goes, a hundred,
maybe a thousand times more-
and it will be this
one day
that makes him sad.

UNDONE

I took it
out again,
set it up
on an easel,
sure that
I wanted to
finish like so
many other
times.

I started it
long ago,
the citrus tones
and asian style
reminded me
how deeply
I had felt.

Shadow Man
and his guitar,
the beauty
of the
Willow World,
silent and in
pain, the two
of them
unsure how to
carry on.

The layers of
painted over

versions of them
would tell
the real tale
if
they could.

At first
they had looked
and longed
for each other
across canvas,
maybe he
more
than her
but still...

Then hurt,
Shadow began
to leave,
and the geisha
watched
sad,
unable to be his,
a tear
as she watched
him go.

Later,
she is painted
in white-
in mourning-
but her
back is turned

to him. She looks
back at the
castle
where she lives
as royalty,
he climbs
the same hill,
his progress
slow
and unsteady.
I would that
I could finish it,
I am unable.

I get it out
and set it
on easel
again,
on this day
you are wed,
and I look
at it.

I look at
you

I look at
me

at the way
I would have
things be,
and I wish
I could have

been more
graceful
in the letting go,
I lay aside
my brush
but I leave
the painting.

It remains undone,
but I will never finish
and it will always remain.

TWILIGHT'S SONG

Long after
the ice had
melted
in his glass
ruining the
potency
of his drink,

he sat at the
keyboard,
staring, wishing
he could
write the
perfect poem.

Long after
the meeting
in past lives
on dusty devil
crossroads
where he had
rushed ahead
to show her,

he ached
in heart
with longing.

If he could
but put
into words

his desires
and passions,
if he could
write the perfect

poem,
he would
tell the world
of her beauty,
the beauty
of her soul.

He would
share the
laughter
that cried out
of him
in the stillness
each time
his mind went
to her,

each time
he wondered
what the
jazz mans daughter
could see
in the dirge
that was his song.

TOGETHER BACK OUT THE DOOR

My life
was a coffee stain
on the living
room carpet
just inside
the front door,
but you were
fresh laundered
bed sheets
sprinkled
with baby powder.

I was pinch
your nose and
take your medicine,
you were
coffee and beignets
at the Cafe Du Monde
on a sexy
sultry morning
and knowing looks
across the table.

I stayed in
and read books
you danced
in flimsy silk
nothings
in the summer
rain

urging me along.
Together
we were stifled
moaning
in the coat room
at a strangers
New Years Eve
party
and laughter
as we
slipped back
out the door.

ALONE

The best
conversation
he ever had
was
through the glass
with his
celly's wife
because that dude
was solid
and felt bad
for anybody
with
no family
or friends.
His days
went
uninterrupted
by television,
or vocation.
His nights
uncorrupted
by pillow
or wife.
He kept
company instead
with a ballet
of words on
the page,
a symphony
of syntax.

Days he
spent with
masters Carver,
Ciardi, Carruth.
Nights,
his own demons,
dark muses
and booze.
These days it
seems
like everybody
knows him,
the parties,
the readings,
the girls.
Snarky banter
with sculptors
and shared
eye rolls
with pompous film makers
and bitches
from CNN.
These days
it all seems
like bullshit.
These days
are for feeling
alone.

MY BURDEN

Like a song
played on an
out of tune
guitar,

like store front
city streets
in dying
southern towns,

like green
hand picked
tattoos blurred-
distorted by time,

the thoughts
that twist
and wrench
through my head
some nights.

Like a newborn pony
I walk uneasy
on shaking legs-

one a.m.

two a.m.

five and six.

I am a dervish,
I paint,
I write,
I cry.

This is what
it is like,

this is my
burden.

HIGH

I set my sights

high

and watched her
singing in a voice
molasses thick
twice as sweet.

Watched as she
coaxed acrylics
and oils into

bold

statements on
canvas stretched
drum-skin tight.

I read her words
shared mine with
her

wept sometimes
at the romance

of unrequited love.

I set my sights
on the most beautiful
girl in the world,
I fell short
but the air was
so sweet
up there.

EASY TO BE THE POEM

It was so easy
to be the poem.

To be the
small town
big family
boy flying
kites in
lonesome
cotton fields.

It was
easy to be
the poem.

To be
the happy man
fresh with love,
in love with
the girl
he met in college
the mother
of children
adored.

So very easy
to be
the poem.

Harder now
it seems
to be the poet.

If the Delta fields
were lonesome
then the grey
city sidewalks
are lonely.

Harder.

The haunting
taunting
memories of
painful separations

foggy flip
stomach mornings-
head pounding-
in line with other
stinking tramps
full of doubt
about the words
that I write.

So much
harder
to be the poet.

The days
spent asking
strangers to reject.
Nights filled
with crumpled pages
and a long slow
dance with
pain and sadness.

And bourbon and dope.

Harder
to be the poet
than the
poem.

WHEN I THINK

When I think
about my childhood
I think of
Saturday mornings
and The Super Friends
and three channels
that we changed
with a pair of pliers,
because the knob
had come off
the television
and got lost.

When I think
of my Mom
I think of
tucking in
hugs and kisses
and french toast
for six kids
made with
an entire loaf of
Wonders.

When I think
of my Dad
I think about
the trips down
gravel roads and
Whistle Bridge
and learning to

shoot guns with
open sights.
When I remember my
brothers and sisters
I smile
and recall
freeze tag,
and softball
and all of us playing
together in the yard.

When I think
of you,
when I drink
too much,
I can only recall
the sadness
of losing
you.

SO BAD

we weep
together
you and i

oughtn't
we be
satisfied

i have left
behind the
blackened spoon

and you
will have your
doctor soon

so why
then
are we sad

we lay
apart the
two of us

we pray to
die and
drink and cuss

when all these things
seem so good
why then do

we feel so bad

I WANTED TO LOVE HER

I was sadder
than a belly up
gold fish floating
in a bowl
on a ten year old
girls dresser
next to an empty
hamster cage.

Over green-eyed
girls, and 80's T.V.
starlets out West.

Over barefoot
beauties cooking
spaghetti and a
wine tipping chick
from a hippy church
with a little boy
who seemed
my own.

Set up by a broad
that ran a gypsy
bistro we had
started to chat.
Here's the deal,
she said
I danced for
thirteen years

Relief or
something like
it washed
over me and I smiled
a crooked grin.
Hell I was
married to a
hooker.

After letting
our guards down
we talked of
silly things,
and drank deeply-
drunk on
the hope of
better days.

We shared melancholy
and music,

Mrs. Beasley and
Mr. French.

God knows she was
older than the girls
from before but
just as beautiful.

She was beautifully sad,
and I wanted to love her.

ANOTHER SUNSET

The air of downtown
hung on us
like chains,
heavy as Marley's sins.

She sat in a chair
by an open window,
her tanned legs crossed
at the ankles,
and hanging out
over a Chester Street sidewalk,
across from a pizza and beer joint
where I read poetry
once a month.

I still had on
yesterdays clothes
and my beers
would get warm
while I watched her
eating frozen grapes.

Just a couple of blocks away
was an Architectural firm
and the upstairs landing
outside its back door
where I used to lay my head.

A couple more past that,
the Salvation Army and

a small crowd of invisibles
waiting for dying day's
last meal.

What are you doing tonight baby?

And I look at her
through the bottom
of a jar like my mother used
to put up vegetables from the garden.

I need to write.

She smiles like
an eight year old who has
managed to trick the
tooth fairy for an extra dime,

When it cools down some
we can get naked and take a nap.

In the tiny kitchen
I reach and open the refrigerator
without standing,
and pour another beer
into the Mason jar,

Sure, baby, sure

and I cannot wait for another sunset.

BUSTED UP HEART AFFAIRS

So, sitting

at the keyboard
when the thought
comes to me.

Scratching
a great scar,
it was five.

Five bypasses
and a valve repair.
All worth it.

Felicia came
and held
my hand.

And Sally
smiled and won
my mother.

Kara brought tacos,
laid down
in my bed,

we talked of lumps,
and heart attacks
and being lousy at love.

I barely remember
Lynne, but she is
an angel.

It came to
me later, sitting
to write.
I was no
more down with
dying

than some
long ago prophet,
my father's book.

I still loved
too many, so many
I'd loved before.

Sitting down
at my keyboard I
wanted to live.

I knew it
would be my
heart though,

would get me one day.

A ROLLIE UPON WAKING

That morning
sitting up
in a never-made
bed, and
rolling a cigarette-
its ends
unkempt with
brown-golden
tobacco
and loose bits
all in his lap-

he thought
of her.
He no longer
gave
a damn.

He thought that
ends of his
rollie looked
like an old man

like him

with hair growing
from his ears,
he thought
of her
and wrote

a poem

because
he no longer
gave
a damn.

ENOUGH

She was not the prettiest
girl in school
but she was still
The Queen.

She held onto her
goods
as long as she could,
then settled
for a husband
she didn't love.

When that
didn't last
she went back
to school
and didn't make
friends,
a 4.0 in the
end.

At 30 she blossomed,
little blue birds
flitted about her head

and every man, woman,
and child fell
in love with
her,

and it was almost
Enough.

LIKE A LITTLE GIRL

the ghost of us
is the only thing
older than the
red and yellow
thai takeout
containers
spilling over
and around
the garbage can
with its living line
of ants
that separate
living room from
kitchen

the stereo
that i found
on the side
of the road
in sherwood
plays a
van morrison cover
and even though
your eyes were blue
it seems
dead on
the drink
in my hand
gone
and the ice
too far away

so i pour
straight from
the bottle
and sink farther
into the past

drinking
alone
to be with you

INTERMISSION

She had
hot shoes
and a slinky
dress that
hugged her bottom
like I wished
I could.

At a Sunday
afternoon
showing
of an opera
at a small town
University

leaning
into each other
caught up
in the sadness
of voices
and strings
I am aroused.

Nothing turns
me on
like sad.

I touched her
silky legs
as gentle

as a spiders
web,
she made
a low purring sound
barely audible
to me
above the oboe.

Slipping out
we found
ourselves
in harmonious
throes
in a public
restroom
while a roll
of tissue
made way
for us
and skipped
out of
sight.

Laughing
in hushed
shooshing
flirtations,

we make
it back to
our seats
in plenty
of time

to push
into each
other

and cry.

THE LOWEST TIME

Baby's in the
bathroom, fixing

her hair. I smoke
yesterdays butts.

My head pounding
and heart sick.

I pretend to read.

My baby girl
calls out "White Boy".

I help her fasten
the cheap necklace

that I got her
all those lows ago.

She pretends to smile.

Reaching towards
her reflection,

I take the last
of a bottle of gin

and toast our love.
She smells like

dollar store perfume
and resignation.
We dance an
awkward little dance
a little stumbly

a little sad

and she says
she has to go.

So I pick up my
book and she

puts on her shoes
and I'll wait for

my Baby to come home.

A NEW POEM

He wasn't
exactly
a hustler

but he had
an easy way
with women

and a hard
time with whiskey
and told a

funny joke.

He never
ever chased them
or even thought...

Sometimes
in the bars they'd
slide on over

and fall
in love with
the words

that he spoke.

With the poems
about other

women.

He would sit
and talk and smile in that
way that he had.

Later, sometimes,
he would take them
to their beds

but it was
only the booze that
he cared for.

The next night
would bring a different
bar, another girl,

a new poem.

PRESTIDIGITATION

You seemed
to love me
from the first
smile.

Enchanted
as I was
by your laughing
eyes,

I was lost
in their
hocus pocus
but

it was
the cut deeply
by life's
Houdini swords
piercing the trunk
escape act;
the rusted razor
circumstance,
on wrists dangling
clinched
white glove
fists,

the bluest smoke
and troublesome
mirrors

of the world
that
made us feel
we had known each other
unending.
Lovers clutch

stretched across
an age of majik
boundless
in time.
Hot blooded passion
coupled oddly
with cold feet
and buttocks,
and under the
covers,
a warmest heart
embrace,

I emptied
myself
into that smile.
Mornings
curtain call-
encore then
cigarettes
and French Press
coffee outside,

slow as abracadabra

then with
no sense of
showmanship or

slight of hand
you told me.
You told me of
your dreams.

I couldn't be
the one.

I said it wouldn't
be fair to
you,

much as I
would love to
live happy
lost
in your Sirens
Spell.

Tomorrows children
must find another
Father,
a better man
than I
had ever been.

Part of me disappears
before your very
eyes,

now you seen-
now you don't:
nothing up my
sleeve.

Out of nothing
disappointed tears-
collateral damage,
of a trick bag
I have never
quite
unpacked.

WHEN WE ARE ROCK STARS

i have a friend

a respectable women

a good wife and mother

who lives in a bastion

of knowledge and wealth

she is kind

of heart and deed

sometimes she comes to see me

AND WE LIVE

LIKE ROCK STARS

there is no limit to our decadence

we eat the richest deserts first then

dinner with heavy sauces

of dairy and drippings

DRINKING WINE

from the bottle without wiping

it's near escape

down our chins

WE SCREW

with reckless abandon

committing unnatural acts

in elevators of hotels

where we are not even guests

we drive to delta riverboats at three a.m.

and play blackjack and craps

I SHAKE DICE and

SHE BLOWS

on them making points the hard way

AND WE DANCE

early or late in clubs with pulsing music too loud to stand

still

AND WE DANCE ALONE

skin touching skin with no
music at all

save what is in our hearts

and then after

THE FINAL CURTAIN

we are ourselves again

until the next time that

WE ARE ROCK STARS

I NEVER WONDER

I never wonder
why you love me
You are so filled
with affection you
cannot contain the magic

Instead I wonder
why you stay.

Why you stay
and listen to my
excuses for losing
another job, and
tell me things will
be better soon

Why you sit quietly
and listen to me
as I drink and
become more brilliant
by the minute
until finally
I am just an ass
who pisses in
the closet not
knowing where
I am.

Why you would
scrap together the
last few dollars

to get me a bottle
even though you
never had a drink
in your life and
could use a new brassiere
because the old one
is worn out and
it's the only one

you've got.

I often wonder at
night after you have
drifted off why it is
that you stay
with a mean old
bastard who
calls himself a poet,
based on the pile
of rejection slips
stacked up
like some great
paper mountain
waiting to be scaled
by only
the bravest souls.

Why, I wonder
do you weep sometimes
when I read my words
aloud to you,
when you are so
tough on the rest

of the world
a lioness with
bared teeth
at the ready

I never wonder
why I keep on loving you

forever,

though I don't
deserve to.

PASSION

soft curves
bosom
and buttocks

tiny beads
of sweat
above candy lips

tops flung
across
the room

jeans hurriedly
escaped one
leg turned out

bed clothes
pushed down
knotted

and no cares
in the world
for now

rhetorical passions
spoken and
answered

GRAND SLAM AND A HOOKER AT THREE A.M.

The saddest guy
I've ever
known
painted 10,000
self portraits
and even
wrote an opera
about his life.
Some days
he'd shave
and be stuck
for hours
trying
to see his
own soul.
In bars,
the others
would crowd
around him:
he would
sing and
tell jokes
and he had a smile
that no one
could look
away from.
To him
women were
like ants
drawn
to the

fresh dropped
and
half melted
ice cream cone
that was
his life.
17 to 70
they all wanted
to save him,
make him better,
fix him.
Only the ones
who were the
most melancholy
appealed to him
and they
just as a way
to look
into the mirror
while sitting
in an orange
vinyl booth
in a darkened
corner
in the back
of Denny's
with the girls
who strolled
in the night.

COMMUNION

Greyhound fresh
with your blues shoes
and backpack
and back home Mama's tears
still damp
on your cheek.

Sun magic outline
city block stare
bus stop aureole
glowing haloed girl
all flower fresh bloomed
and debit card and blood of the lamb.

Drifting up to you
gently as smoke,
vacating shadows
I take your burden
over my shoulder
all Lucky Strikes and grave dirt
and one third of the stars.

Melancholy moccasins
keeping time with
black, buckled beat boots
to Main Street Liquor
and four fifty pints
on a dirty grey blanket.

And sunset by the river
shoulder to shoulder
beneath celestial ceiling
we share
Pamplona, and Picasso and Paradise Lost
and potted meat.

Crossing our fingers
we fall in love
a little
for the briefest moment in time.

City scape illumination
reflected in
rushing waters
like Vincent's blurry stars.

At dawn
my boots back on
I will walk you again
to a bus stop pilgrimage
to anywhere next
but my quick broken heart
is rooted

to Downtown mornings here
and my favorite bars
on a sidewalked city street
named for Bill.

TO THE WHORE WHO RUINED MY LIFE

A deal breaker
you said

if he doesn't
understand
the relationship
we share.

Beauty and the Beast
connection.

Poet and Muse.

You dance through
my mind now,
you said.

Tell me you would
fuck my eyes out,
you said,

angelic face
crimson,
an X-rated grin.

Suddenly
nothing;
no peep,

not even
superficial
kindness.

A heart-crushing
headhunter.

A killer of
men's souls.

Having been prey
to you,

I pray
you curse your
God
and kill yourself.

Hell,
I'll split it
with you.

I already
curse God
for you.

I should
tell
you I
lied too.

Your poetry
is trite,
garbage really.

I could never
say it

while caught
in hypnotic
cobra's gaze;

couldn't tell
you
your lines
held no sway,

when we were

more,

before

my life

was ruined.

SLEEPING GIRL

Having yanked
down the mildewed
shower curtain
while
pissing blood
or Red Stripe

or whatever

and stumbling
back to a
half crumbled
pack of Kools

on her

side of the bed,
he began to
study her
sleeping face,
her other-worldly

beauty.

He stood wooden
just for
a moment,
and thought
that she was
the one he
had loved.

Having pissed,
and smoking
a Kool,
(he hated menthols)
he wondered
if he were
the only one
who sold out
and settled,

for Jamaican beer,
and shitty smokes,

and a lonely girl

he didn't know.

A CERTAIN KIND

In those days
he was
just
beginning to be
noticed,
and they
would come
to him,

often
a student from
the local university,
sometimes
a Muse,
occasionally
rarely,
a protegee

and they
would
pretend to love
him
and he them.

Flash fire
hot and fast.

Sweat and bruises
and sweet juices.

Tender

trailing fingertips
dirty talk

but it was

the inevitable
break-up,

tears and
curses.
The self-loving
heart-ache
that he craved.

YOUR POEMS SUCK!

shouted the best
of them,
the ones who
knew how to cut

as he
painted them out
of pictures,
gave waitresses
the pet names
he'd always called
them.

And drunk
on the petty
drama
of the

broken hearted,
he'd wander
blindly down
dirty streets.

Tickle the lock
of the boarding house
door
and enter
the smothering
silence.

Addicted,

he'd say
to himself
and sit
at the keyboard
lit by shabby
single lamp
and peck away
at the night

again.

I DON'T NEED YOU

I don't need you
to love me.

I just want
(to love)
you.

I want to be
the sun shining
on your face,

the rain that
traces your
cheek

while you
dance,
spinning in

warmest
spring downpour,
laughing.

I don't want
to swim in
your passion.

I would drown
in your soul,
arms weak- chest bursting.

I don't need
you to love me,
I just need you
to let me love
you.

JOELLA TURNED TRICKS

before I met her
and only
sometimes after
like when she was
mad at me or
maybe herself.
we did dope together
at first but
eventually just drank,
such was our love.
her mother died
too soon, and
father was a monster.
he used her.
and his friends.
finally he set her
on fire with zippo
lighter fluid and
scarred her outside too.
we were hurt;
her as a child
me, less so, by
life and a bad
first marriage
we clung
to each other
like a cobweb
to an out of reach
corner,
such was our love.
we told each

other secrets,
drunk late at night,
sharing tears,
and fears
and passions.
A fiery sunset
beautiful but
for a moment
then gone,

such was our love.

WE TALKED OF COLERIDGE

She taught English
second semester
of my senior year.
Straight from the University,
she seemed so
enlightened.
I believe it's called a crush.
We talked
of Byron and Coleridge,
she smiled
at my enthusiasm.
She offered me
the Beat Generation,
and I was in love.
She asked me to write,
I filled reams.
i copied e.e.'s style,
stole subjects from Ginsberg.
I tried to find my angst.
I utilized adolescent innuendo,
and it seemed to work.
We met at coffee shops,
and I ordered espresso
served in a tiny cup and saucer.

She had a soda.

The things that she taught me,
the words that we shared...

Xanadu.

I TOLD HER I LOVED HER

For all
of my days-
in every
kind of
storm,
I will remember
the night I
said it
out loud.

Riding a
rocket of
a few more
than I should
Diamond Bear
beers from the
the cooler
and a cheerful
crowd for
my lines,

we stood on
a downtown
sidewalk
littered with
cigarette butts
and past hope
dreams.

She held me
in those
fucking

rain forest-
green eyes.

Rapt.
I do,
I do.
I really do
love you...

I don't
want you,

well I do

but I don't
expect
anything.

Hell, the
damn thing
works better
if you don't...

I just want
to write you
ten thousand
love poems.

She smiled
and that
was good
enough
for me.

SEASONS

Our story
will be
a beautiful
one.

It will
span our
lifetimes
and seasons
hot and
cold.

I will
offer you
myself,
the real me,
but you
choose instead
the poet.

I will
always send
you love poems
and you

will write
love poems to me
saying
you can't love me
that way.

And people
will see our love-
love better, for our words.

And we will write
a beautiful romance.

I ask for
a lover
you offer me
a muse.

And when
my words have
all been written

selfishly

I hope you
are there

with me.

LOVE POEM YOU SHOULDN'T WRITE FOR VALENTINES

Listen,
I am not saying
that you are

not great,

I mean
you are.
You tell me
you love me,

show me,

you work hard
at your job
come home
and cook.

I am
just saying
that sometimes
I need
a little more-

for Christ's sake

turn a trick
or something.

Screw the
neighbor

then tell me
it didn't
mean a thing.
Shoot at me
when I
come home drunk
or at least
throw
my coffee cup

full

of boiling joe
at my face
while I ignore
you mornings,
caught up
in poems by

Raymond Carver.

I don't want
to hurt you
but I am a poet

and Holy Crap

I kind of have
a reputation.

I can't be
writing love poems
all the time.

KRYPTONITE

I am not Super,
the earths yellow
sun
makes my head
pound
some mornings.

As a boy I
would use
clothespins to
fasten Moms
bath towels
around my
neck.

Close as I
ever got.

Still those
eyes,
like Kryptonite,
make me
weak

steal my ability
to speak

then

make me repeat
myself; ramble.

Caught in the

tractor beam
of her smile

I cannot
I am fearful

that Scotty
will
snatch me
from her
in a swirl
of color and
light,

before I tire of
her world.

I never tire
of her world,

or those
Kryptonite eyes.

I am not
Superman,

still
in her presence

I would leap
buildings;

at least make
a bounding try.

SHE ALWAYS STAYED

Some days listening
to upbeat hillbilly tunes
he'd smile a wrinkled grin
and be dumb
at how sprung she had
made him,
but then the smile
remained,
and he remembered
how damn good
she had made him feel
on better days.

He would think of the others:
the lesbians, and the catfish,
the ones with ten perfect toes
and how none could live up
to faded freckles on her nose,
and he would smile
some more and go back
to her.

Remembering late
night poetry
on glowing cell phone screen

and later how he had thought
he might die pining
as pathetic as a teen.

He would smile and put her away,
to enjoy another day.
Again and forever
just like she had always stayed.

BUT ONE

He wrote the
myth of
himself
every time
the story danced out
of his mouth
on bourbon scented
breath.

He had a shock
of untamed hair,
and a bullet-proof
countenance
that was pleasant
enough
but it was the words-

his self-proclaimed
legend-

and the colors
that he painted them-

with deft
brushstrokes
of sweet tea

sinful flirtations
in graveled
Southern drawl,
that made them
want him.

She was a
Christ church woman.
A singer of praise,
gifted with angelic spirit,
a soulful
doorway to
Gods own throne,
her heavenly form
that of a
girl
perpetually
fresh blossomed,
slender and soft.

Hanging on his
musings
she would
smile at him
with her
eyes;

greenest gems
of exotic
faraway lands,
glued to every
foolish thing
he'd do.

They shared time
in stolen moments.

He was not her man.

Together
they breathed in
the arts,
and music

and a love of love
or at least
it's game.
And she would

share her joys with him

and other times her pain.

Softened
he would tell
her of his
broken life;
a dark
and twisted tale
of lost love
and pin prick
highs.

I wonder how
many have fallen
in love with you.

All of them,
he'd say
a Superman smile,

and she thought

it might be
true.

The short lived
romance
a screeching tire
car flight
through heavy traffic
dangerous and loud

and lastly a
twisted heap of burning
metal-

the wreckage
of reckless lust.
10,000
bottles later,
and nearly as many
poems,

he'd
recall her,
fondly,

all of them but one.

ABOUT THE AUTHOR

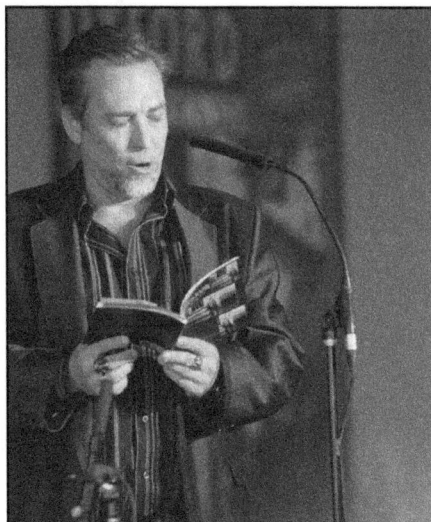

Justin Booth lives and works in Little Rock, AR. He suffers a quick-broken heart and has been diagnosed with a mental health disorder. The latter resulting in years of self-medicating and homelessness, the former poetry and sad stories. He has published three collections of poetry: "Hookers, Ex-Wives and Other Lovers," "Trailer Park Troubadour" and "Lucky Strikes, Grave Dirt and 1/3 of the Stars."

A former drug addict and state prison inmate, Booth gives a poetic voice to the often ignored urban South. He talks of beauty in the ugliest places, the despair of absolute poverty and the redemption of the human spirit.

His plain spoken style and hypnotic use of meter allow us to join him in a bittersweet journey to places we have never been before.

 # the luckiest man

On Twitter @ OutlawPoet1